The Great Millennium Floods
in
Kent and Sussex

Compiled by Kathy Leeds

WATER, water everywhere ... it poured from the sky, washed over fields and roads into villages and towns, and put Kent-Sussex border country into the national spotlight - more of a bog garden than the Garden of England in the great millennium floods.

This is the story of dramatic rescues, lucky escapes, devastation for households and businesses, and amid the chaos a strong community spirit as people helped each other through.

Kathy Leeds, feature writer for Courier Newspapers, has compiled The Great Millennium Floods in Kent and Sussex using reports and pictures in the Courier as the basis.

This book contains many hitherto unpublished pictures and stories, together with some of the more dramatic pictures of devastation, and beauty, from the papers. Kathy has talked to both flood victims and rescue services, and looked at the history of flooding in this part of southern England.

The Great Millennium Floods in Kent and Sussex is a record of four extraordinary weeks of weather and their consequences.

Acknowledgements

The following are thanked for their contributions to this book:

The Photographers: Gary Francis, Gavin Sawyer, Arthur O'Hara, Paul Viney, Katherine Coulstock, Kirk Lee, Faith Lee and Samantha Rousell.

We are also grateful to Norman Rogers for his pictures on pages 3 and 9; Clive Warrender (page 44), Nigel Bowles, John Connors Press Associates (pages 30, 31 and 33); Kent News and Pictures (pages 37 and 38); Solent News and Photo Agency (page 8); Michael Brophy (pages 26-28); Dorothy Highwood (page 51); Eden Valley Museum.

The Met Office provided the charts on pages 6 and 7.

The history: Frank Chapman for the section on flooding history in Kent and Frank Sellens for the chapter on past flooding in East Sussex.

Technical assistance: Stuart Webber, Roger Blackford, Sally Taylor and James Bushell.

The Courier newsgathering team: Darrel Billingham, Emily Pennink, Jennifer Pickering, Katherine Jacques, Trisha Fermor, Louise Ford, Libby Sutcliffe, James Drury, Kate Murrell, Mary Harris, Richard White, Yvonne Gordon.

The Kent and Sussex Police Forces and the Kent and East Sussex Fire Brigades.

ISBN 0-9539832-0-X

©Courier Printing and Publishing Company Ltd 2000

Published by the Courier Printing and Publishing Co Ltd, Longfield Road, Tunbridge Wells, Kent, TN2 3HL
Printed by Henry Ling Ltd, The Dorset Press, Dorchester, DT1 1HD

Front and back cover pictures: the village of Yalding in Kent.

It seemed the rain would never stop...

Rain, rain, and yet more rain - in that second week of October 2000 it seemed it would never stop.

It poured down relentlessly over Kent and Sussex from leaden skies, until it had nowhere left to go in sodden countryside which could take no more.

Ditches, streams and rivers were overwhelmed by the deluge. Sheets of murky brown water spread across fields, then boiled under bridges and over roads where natural or built landscape concentrated its force.

Normally mild-mannered little rivers barged their way into communities sending filthy torrents into homes and businesses. Courier country was suddenly making national headline news as the millennium floods surged downstream.

Emergency services scrambled to respond to the natural disaster, and it brought the novel sight of lifeboats plying the main streets of country towns and villages. It gave a new meaning to inshore rescue - more an on-shore rescue, miles inland from the coast.

In Sussex, Uckfield found television fame as the River Uck surged through the High Street, as did Kent villages of Lamberhurst, invaded by the Teise, and Yalding, inundated by the combined efforts of the rivers Medway, Teise and Beult.

The far larger town of Tonbridge held its breath on the Medway upstream, waiting to see if the Leigh

Rivers which were normally mild-mannered barged their way into communities sending filthy torrents into businesses and homes

flood barrier would do its job: it did - just. Downstream the Kent county town of Maidstone watched anxiously as the river levels rose.

Back in Sussex floodwaters swept on from Uckfield and swelled the River Ouse which swamped the county town of Lewes in conjunction with high tides. Residents were evacuated, emergency centres were set up.

There were reports of rescues, lucky escapes, and heartache and misery for householders and traders, who saw their belongings and stock vanish underwater - some not for the first time this year.

By the Thursday afternoon the rain was clearing, and Friday 13th brought blue skies and brilliant sunshine in which the stunned population could view the devastation.

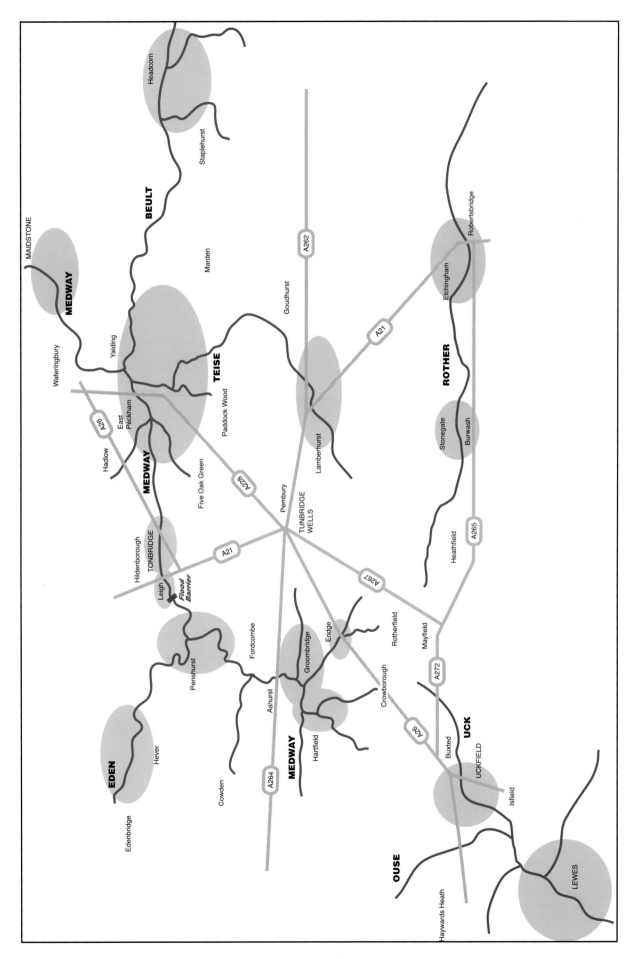

Areas affected by the millennium year floods in West Kent and East Sussex.

4

A Blitz spirit prevailed as people rallied to help each other in worst-hit areas, and elsewhere people went to gaze amazed at the suddenly changed landscape. Older residents had memories of flood disasters past, from the 1960s, even the 1940s. Younger people had known nothing like it on this scale across two counties.

But this was the worst flooding that had been seen in Kent and Sussex for over 50 years.

As the water, tainted with sewage and fuel, slowly subsided the lengthy task of cleaning up began, counting the cost in terms of furniture, fittings and foodstuffs ruined under a coating of brown sludge.

In the modern world where people like to believe they are in control of so much of life, the forces of nature provided a reminder of their awesome power, and the helplessness of mankind in the face of it.

Little did we realise that nature had not yet finished.

Our book tells the story.

Vicky Grant and Stephanie Ogden test the depth of water as they carefully clamber out of Orchard View Stores in Yalding

Please drive carefully, urged the sign, and it was never more appropriate than on October 12, 2000.

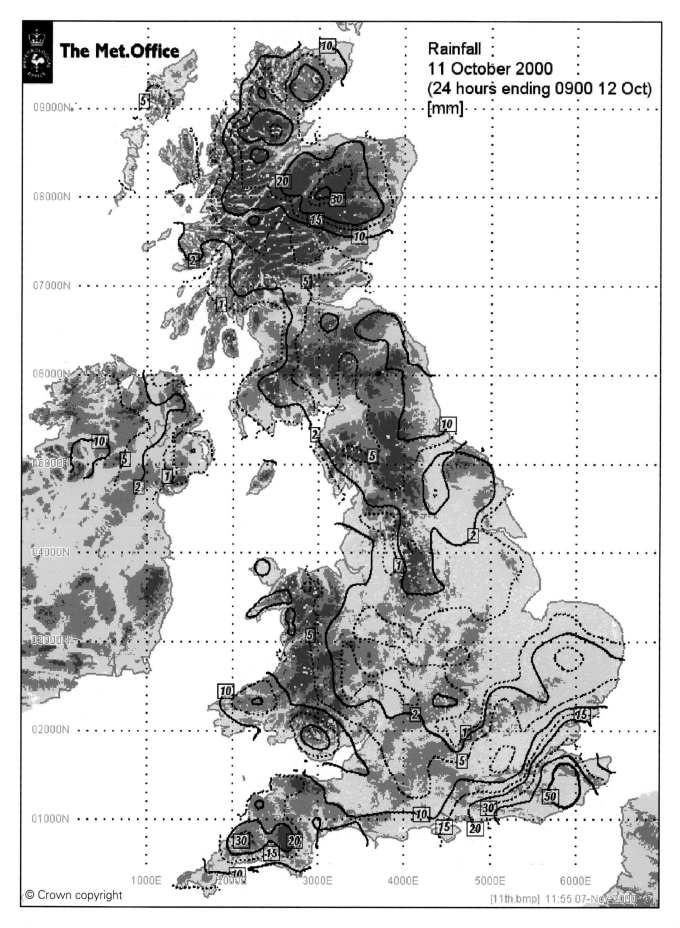

The Met.Office

Rainfall
11 October 2000
(24 hours ending 0900 12 Oct)
[mm]

© Crown copyright

[11th.bmp] 11:55 07-Nov-2000

The centre of the deluge which unleashed over 50mm in 24 hours shows up clearly over Kent and Sussex.

6

Met Office forecasts wetter winters ahead

Seeds of the disaster were sown in a soggy September, according to the Meteorological Office, with unsettled weather from the middle of the month.

Then October became the second wettest since records began in 1766.

In its second week from Monday to Thursday 111.2mm of rain (about 4.5 inches) was recorded at Herstmonceux in Sussex, the nearest weather station, almost two inches of that on the Wednesday night alone.

There was a lull for a week as mopping up began, before another three-quarters of an inch (18.8mm) fell on Friday October 20. Another lull came in the last week of the month but by the Thursday it was known something nasty was brewing out in the Atlantic.

An area of deep low pressure swung in from the ocean, gathering moisture all the way.

"The system had a lot of energy with very strong winds," said a Met Office spokesman. "It was gusting between 60 and 70 mph in the area, though 98mph was recorded at The Mumbles. It was the worst since the 1990 storm, but came on the back of three weeks of rain."

Another 3.5 inches (90mm) of rain was enough to put Lamberhurst and Yalding under water again, but the weather had still not finished. The wind picked up again as November began and by Thursday it was clear another depression was on its way towards Britain to give a Bonfire Night to remember.

October is renowned for depressions but it is not usual to have large storms so close together

"That is what is unusual," the Met Office said. "October is renowned for depressions, but it is not usual to have large storms so close together. The centre of the second low pressure went through the English Channel with winds and rain circulating round it."

Herstmonceux recorded the highest rainfall in the south east in 24 hours from 3pm on that Sunday, 48.4mm being almost two inches. Uckfield High Street was swamped again, and Yalding had its third dose in a month, earning the title on one news bulletin "the unluckiest village in England".

There was talk of the weather events being evidence of the effects of global warming and the Met Office agrees.

"We are beginning to see greater frequency in this, and that ties in with what our climate change experts are saying. We will have wetter winters, heavier and more frequent rainfall. It will affect how we live in future, where we live, and what crops we grow."

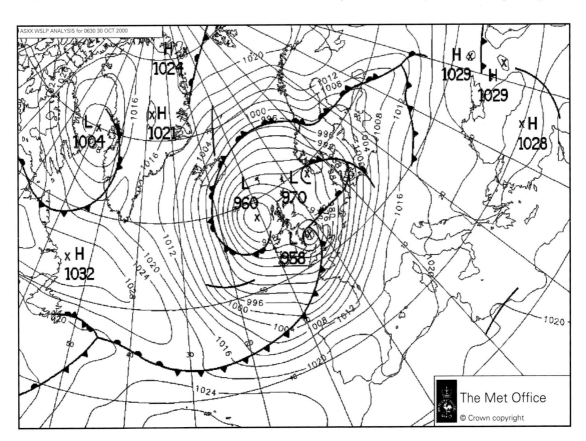

Passage of the October 29 storm illustrated by this depression map.

Uckfield under water on the morning of October 12, 2000.   Picture by Dan Charity (Solent News and Photo Agency)

Uckfield: where trouble began at 6.30am

TROUBLE began for Uckfield early on the morning of Thursday October 12, and by 6.30am the town centre was under a torrent of water four or five feet deep.

Shop windows smashed under its force and stock was swept out into the street, a tangle of food, clothes, videos, from different premises, and some proprietors and staff were stranded while trying to save their goods.

Residents awoke to the sight and sound of a coastguard helicopter hovering above them. Early morning radio and television news bulletins were reporting that a man had been swept away.

Jeweller Vernon Bishop was lucky to be alive after being swept almost a mile downstream before being plucked to safety by a coastguard helicopter. A handful of other pedestrians were helped by brave residents when they were swept off their feet.

RNLI lifeboats used the streets as waterways to rescue people trapped in shops and industrial premises, assisted by the fire brigade.

The town was sealed off by police for most of the day.

Shop windows were smashed under the force of the water and stock was washed out into the street

Few roads were open, most of them being under several feet of water.

Hundreds of people turned out to stand and watch a sight that was as awe-inspiring as it was devastating.

The water reached bar height in the Cock and Bull pub, and round in Bell Lane the fire station was under three feet of water, its bay doors buckled. McDonald's was a submerged island. Shops in Bell Walk suffered the same fate.

The industrial estate was awash, staff who reached work early were trapped by the flood tide. It brought special heartache for businessman Christopher Macklin, just two days after he reopened his Trading

Balanced on a wall near the junction of Bell Lane and High Street, Uckfield, resident Norman Rogers used a digital camera to capture both this, and the McDonald's picture on page 3. These pictures of devastation were taken at 8am on Thursday, October 12, and the one above clearly shows the raging torrent forging across the High Street.

Retired Telecom manager Norman Rogers enjoys photography as a hobby and working with pictures on his computer. Enhancing old family photographs to contemporary quality is one of his skills.

His digital picture of McDonald's in Uckfield, surrounded by water, will be remembered for years to come.

Both McDonald's and Catering Magazine requested use of his shot of the restaurant and an enlargement is now on display at the rebuilt McDonald's in Bell Lane, Uckfield.

"Young children were standing nearby when I took those pictures and I was worried because the current was unbelievable. I used to be in the Merchant Navy and I have seen some huge seas, but in a small area like that even I was impressed."

Some of the cars at Caffyns showroom were submerged, windscreen wipers set off by the water on one of them. In total 19 cars were affected, and the majority were sent to a special flood auction. As a precaution staff took to moving vehicles up-site each night in the wake of the flood. The branch was re-opened for business within days.

Tressler Trailers on the Bellbrook industrial estate lost 22 cars which were written off for the crusher after being contaminated by the water. Business owner of 30 years Jim Manning said the total insurance claim was about £500,000. Goldsmiths and Allcorn had used cars outside under a foot of water, and 12 were write-offs.

Altogether more than a hundred shops and businesses suffered damage and destruction in the October 12 deluge

4U discount warehouse following a £400,000 refit, in the wake of a fire five weeks earlier.

Cars at Caffyns garage were submerged, and two cars were swept out of flooded Mill Lane into the High Street. It was the worst flood in town for 50 years, but not the first this year to put Uckfield on national television news - nor would it be the last.

Altogether more than a hundred shops and business premises suffered damage and destruction in the October 12 deluge. Some managed to re-open within days, others will not be open for several months.

McDonald's brought in a new drive thru/restaurant by road, lifted it into place by crane, and was back in business in 13 days.

Lifeboats were called in from the coast to rescue people trapped in shops, flats and businesses surrounded by floodwater.

When the waters went down, as quickly as they had risen, Uckfield resembled a war zone with its boarded-up shop windows, debris in the streets and damage to the pavements.

Goods from the shops were washed downstream and turned up as far away as Isfield and Barcombe.

Police stayed on duty all night to prevent looting from the damaged properties.

Just three weeks later after the Bonfire Night deluge, as the town was beginning to pick up the pieces, traders and residents could hardly believe that the river was back in the High Street as it broke its banks yet again.

Not so much water went through the High Street this time and only a small number of shops were affected. For some it was a time of despair.

For weeks the lower part of the High Street was sandbagged each night as traders did the best they could to protect their property.

Lucky to be alive after being swept away

Jeweller Vernon Bishop described to Prince Edward and to Uckfield Mayor Cllr Mike Skinner how he was rescued by a coastguard helicopter after being swept away by the force of the water.

No stranger to floods in Uckfield, he had been at his shop, in the north wing of historic Bridge Cottage, from 2am, trying to bail out water a foot or two deep at the start. He was moving valuable computers and stock as high as he could.

When it became pointless five hours later he struggled to keep his head above water and unlock the door below the surface. After clinging to the door frame, he decided to let go and take his chances.

Several hundred yards downstream his cries for help were heard behind the house of Chris Davies in Anvil Close.

Vernon was spotted soaked and shaking on an island in a railway cutting, and airlifted to safety by coastguard helicopter, taking him to Princess Royal Hospital at Haywards Heath.

Meanwhile his son Sebastian had arrived in Uckfield to answer his father's telephone call to help move stock to safety and he knew his father had to still be in the shop, despite the raging torrent of water.

He was relieved to hear from the emergency services that his father had been rescued and, remarkably, suffering only from hypothermia.

Prince Edward was one of several high-profile visitors who came to see the chaos for themselves, and

Prince Edward visited Uckfield to meet the victims and see the devastation as the Environment Agency declared 'We will never tame nature but we must try to minimise the risk'

to commiserate. They included Government minister Elliot Morley who said there might not be an obvious engineering solution to flooding, and Environment Agency chairman Sir John Harman who said it was an "extraordinary" disaster and there was no guarantee of safety against floods.

Sussex area manager for the agency Peter Midgely, who visited the town several times, said the deluge overwhelmed defences, and events and their cause were being examined, adding: "We will never tame nature, but we must try to minimise the risk."

Businesses took no chances for several weeks, sandbagging their doors each night and moving vehicles to high ground.

Lifeboats used the streets as waterways

Nice day for a paddle - rescuers take a breather moored outside the Cock and Bull pub in Uckfield, well into the 36-hour emergency which saw fire crews called in from as far afield as Hastings, Bexhill and West Sussex, and boats were as much in operation as appliances.

Station Commander Dave Sutton said resources were stretched over an area from Robertsbridge through towards East Grinstead in the first flood. "The whole of the Weald was under water that day," he said. The rescue log runs into hundreds and on country roads around villages like Buxted and Barcombe a number of people were snatched from stranded cars in the nick of time.

This 40-year weather event (the last similar scale flooding was in the 1960s) cost East Sussex Fire Brigade three major appliances (value £130,000 new), an operational support unit and several light support vehicles and vans.

Lifeboats were called miles inland to work with the fire brigade crews tackling the disaster.

A crew from Eastbourne saved the lives of six children, swept away into five feet of murky water, while playing near the railway line.

One of the rescuers said they were silly to be playing near the line, dangerous at the best of times.

The youngsters aged between 11 and 13 were all in shock and the consequences could have been much worse.

RNLI personnel and firemen take a breather after rescuing all the trapped people from shops, flats and industrial premises in Uckfield on October 12.

12

Pub where water reached the top of the bar

High water mark inside the Cock and Bull left these machines in the drink and manager Nigel Bean with a major clean-up task.

He had been at the pub for 14 weeks and said: "I have never seen anything like it before. This end of the town is like a ghost town - it has ripped the heart out of it."

Cost of righting the damage to the pub was put between £120,000 and £140,000. The builders called the morning after the Bonfire Night storm to see if their early work had been ruined by the second flood but it had escaped.

"We sat up all night but by 6am it was clear the water was not going to cross the road," said Nigel.

His re-opening was planned for December 3, after losing nine weeks' business in closure, and one of the first events scheduled was a charity night to benefit the fire brigade and the flood relief fund.

I have never seen anything like it before: this end of the town is like a ghost town – Nigel Bean, landlord of the Cock and Bull pub

Supermarket devastated by raging torrent

Inside Somerfield checkouts were awash with food stock which was also washed into the street, through windows shattered by the force of the water, and trapped against railings.

More than £400,000 worth was destroyed, along with equipment valued at more than £1.5million.

But with 10 dehumidifiers working on drying out, closure rumours were quashed by the announcement of a £2million refit with a new store plan.

Firefighter Steve Burgoyne was invited to re-open the refitted store, after almost becoming a victim himself during the search for jeweller Vernon Bishop.

Security CCTV footage caught the drama as firemen tied cables to pillars outside the store to attach safety lines. Steve vanished under swirling water laden with debris, but was saved by his colleagues.

Store manager Mark Taylor said the incident underlined the bravery of the emergency services.

Welcome to Uckfield Station! These two cars and a shed met up in the torrent, with the signal box in the background.

Clothing from Peacocks made a soggy washing line draped over the street railings, entangled with stock from other shops as the water level dropped in the High Street. Shopfitters had just finished refurbishment when new flooring, carpet and resprayed wall panels were wrecked three weeks later by the river returning after the Bonfire Night deluge - on the day new clothes stock was due to be installed.

Humour survived the deluge as near a solitary office chair abandoned by the receding waters was this supermarket sign "Caution. Wet floor".

Against the odds this classic Mini survived its swamping, despite being thought to be a write-off initially.

Thanks largely to a lack of complicated modern electrics, after drying it out, its owners were able to coax it back to life in the days that followed.

Here it comes – residents watch in disbelief as the water swirls into Alexandra Road, Uckfield, lapping round the front door of number 80. Children found delight in paddling in the bigger than usual puddles.

Huge crowds gathered throughout the day to watch the amazing spectacle in Uckfield High Street and police set up roadblocks around the town. Meanwhile the rain continued to fall for most of the day.

The force of the water smashed all the windows in Blockbuster Video, Bell Walk, Uckfield, washing videos downstream as far as Isfield and Barcombe.

The morning after – as the waters receded the damage could clearly be seen.

Coracle proved a sturdy craft in the floods

Ancient methods of transport were one of the best methods of getting through Uckfield as Charlie Quinnell was quick to find out.

Charlie, an A-level student at Uckfield Community College, builds coracles in his spare time and is planning to set up a business in the Hebrides and via the internet.

He became fascinated by the craft during his primary school years at Skippers Hill School and made his first one a year ago.

Crafted from hazel and willow branches and covered with calico and bitumatic paint the coracle proved more stable than a normal boat.

Charlie used his prototype, covered with a tarpaulin instead of calico, to ferry half a dozen desperate people across a footpath which was under five feet of water during the first Uckfield flood.

"They saw the water and said they had to get across," he said. "I also towed a few people to safety who were in dinghies without oars."

He then spent an enjoyable day testing his craft on the flood-filled roads.

Charlie is planning to go on a course at Ironbridge soon where he will learn even more ancient crafts including making rustic furniture, bows and arrows and everything possible from wood, plus hedge-laying.

After his A-levels he is going to learn Gaelic in Scotland before setting up home in the Hebrides.

Charlie plans a coracle making business after his experiences in the floods

Modest heroes Ian Shears and Bill Chapman, pictured with their families, saved a woman from being swept away by the torrent. The woman was trying to walk to work on the Bellbrook industrial estate, Uckfield, when she lost her footing and fell. Ian and Bill snatched her to safety and made sure she was unhurt before continuing on their way.

The crowds came throughout the day on October 12, unable to believe their eyes. Stories were exchanged and tales of bravery recounted, while older residents recalled previous floods in days gone by.

Bell Walk, Uckfield, began to emerge as the flood receded, resembling first a paddling pool, and then revealing the power of the water as its toll of surface damage appeared.

The damage left by the water resembled a war zone as this picture beside the car park in Bell Walk, Uckfield, shows.

Fourteenth century Bridge Cottage, headquarters of the Uckfield and District Preservation Society, lived up to its title and survived yet another inundation in its history. Uckfield's oldest building has come through every flood unscathed since it was built in about 1380. Originally scheduled for demolition to make way for the Uckfield bypass link road, it was bought by the town for £20,000 in 1985 following a public appeal.

The footpath between Somerfield and LloydsTSB became a torrent of water as the River Uck broke its banks, lifting a skip and carrying it up against the LloydsTSB fence. Stock from Somerfield is piled up against the railings.

Uckfield Mill is surrounded by water at the height of the flood. Mill Lane has totally disappeared.

Aftermath: the River Uck has fallen back to more normal levels but leaves evidence of its destruction in Mill Lane, Uckfield.

Sixteen-year-old Peter Funnell saved the first three months of his wages during the summer to buy a video camera. He was on the scene as the waters rose and has dramatic shots of Uckfield jeweller Vernon Bishop being airlifted to safety by coastguard helicopter and the Somerfield windows bursting open under the weight of a tidal wave of water and stock.

"The window of Somerfield's went with a terrific bang and everything poured out," he said.

Bridget Matthews clearing flood debris from the cafe in Bell Walk, behind Bridge Cottage, Uckfield.

Minor roads around Buxted, including Pound Lane, here, east of Framfield, were no match for the floods. A small Wealden District Council truck got out of its depth in Sandy Lane, Framfield. Buxted was almost cut off by the water, reaching a depth of 5ft in places. Drivers who gambled on getting through abandoned waterlogged cars on the roads.

Some residents were evacuated by lifeboat, and cellar contents were ruined at the White Hart pub as water poured in.

Afternoon sunlight and blue skies are reflected in the calm of a new lake which had been created near Streele Farm, north of Framfield. While the floods caused despair for many they also created picture postcard scenes like this.

Rother and Dudwell rivers take their toll

Further East from Uckfield the rivers Rother and Dudwell were adding their waters to the misery of East Sussex residents, joining together at Etchingham before surging on to Robertsbridge.

Upstream at Stonegate the road was cut by the floods, and at Burwash residents in Shrub Lane had their homes awash to a depth of 9ft at worst. The lowest point of the valley at Crowhurst Bridge Farm saw torrents of water engulf an unoccupied residential barn.

Three gaping holes were washed out under the railway tracks at Etchingham, deep enough for engineers to stand in, unable to see out. Stations down the line from Wadhurst to Hastings were shut for four days as 17,000 tons of ballast were brought in to plug the gap in a round-the-clock repair project.

Minor roads in the Etchingham area were impassable, and the second lashing of wind and rain at the end of October was enough to convince the owners of the village stores to call it a day after a year in business which ended with the ground floor and storage areas under water, destroying stock.

Some families moved out of the village to wait for their homes to dry.

Etchingham: the station resembled a canal

Etchingham railway station (right) resembled a canal scene (below left), not a train in sight, and cars were drowned in the car park (below).

No through road – rising floodwater at Etchingham made minor roads like this one impassable.

Etchingham parish church of the Assumption of Blessed Mary and St Nicolas was unluckily flooded, about two feet deep through the nave, up steps into the chancel and reaching the altar steps.

Water was in the spaces under the choir stalls, and three or four feet deep in the boiler room. At the west end the vestry was flooded and the lower portion of the newly-restored organ, more than £5,000 of work finished less than a year ago.

Historic brasses of the Etchingham family, who founded the church in 1372, were under water on the chancel floor, as were Sussex rarity encaustic medieval tiles, which will need specialist treatment. The upright piano was ruined, some wall-hangings were caught by the water, but most of the old needlework hassocks were safe because they were up on the pews.

The building was expected to be closed for six months for drying out, with Easter the hopeful target for resuming full services, possibly January for spoken services without music.

Etchingham medieval parish church was the only church outside Lewes to be flooded – about two feet deep through the nave

Rain stops play at Robertsbridge

Rain stopped play at this Robertsbridge playground during the floods. Garden furniture swept down the High Street as 4ft waves poured through, swamping homes and shops and causing thousands of pounds worth of damage.

Electricity was also cut off for 48 hours, the village plunged into darkness.

People were stunned by the speed and the depth of the water, and elderly resident Edith Dando told how she awoke to find the water armpit-deep downstairs.

Her first thought was to get pets safely upstairs, but there was no time to rescue personal possessions.

The second flood in three weeks at the end of October damaged some High Street properties and saw Northbridge Street and Rutley Close under water.

The parish council chairman reported that some residents had just finished cleaning up from the first flood, and were getting "very depressed", worrying about the future. Some thoughts had turned to moving, but it would not be easy to sell flood-prone property.

Floods through the site, up to four-and-a-half feet deep in the warehouse, were the second dose of bad luck to hit cricket bat makers Gray Nicholls in Robertsbridge this year after its museum was damaged by fire in the roof back in June.

Sales director Richard Gray was pictured then amid the debris. Old brochures dating back to founding of the company in 1855 were ruined, but fortunately most of the bat collection was on the ground floor and the most valuable were saved.

In the floods the factory became "like a river", and an extensive clean-up operation was needed afterwards to tackle the silting, according to Mr Gray. The company lost materials and machinery, and office items, plus four weeks working before it was back in partial production.

Rescuers themselves were in danger at one point when six lifeboat crew narrowly escaped as their boat was dragged under Cliffe Bridge in Lewes while searching for two missing children (who turned up safe).

Onlookers screamed warnings as strong currents bounced the boat against the side of the bridge. The men scrambled up just seconds before the craft vanished, but one crewman toppled into the water and was plucked to safety by his colleagues before he too was sucked under. An eyewitness said: "I was sure he was going to drown. It was a close shave - these guys are all heroes."

Pictures: Nigel Bowles, John Connor Press Associates

Cordoned off until the waters go down: Lewes pedestrian shopping precinct looking towards the Cliffe bridge.

An air of disbelief hung over Lewes

HISTORIC county town Lewes bore the brunt of floodwaters from the River Uck joining the swollen Ouse, at the time of high coastal tide. An air of disbelief hung over the town as the extent of the devastation began to sink in.

A whole month's rainfall had fallen in three days, and people were stunned by the sheer volume of water and the speed of its rising. In the lower part of the town, homes, cars, and businesses were swamped. Some were evacuated by boat, others moved upstairs trying to save what possessions they could. Some escaped with only the clothes they stood up in.

Emergency services liaised under a gold command situation, co-ordinated by the police whose headquarters remained above the flood limit - and provided temporary base for the ambulance service which was not so lucky.

The fire brigade also had to battle its own flood, with the control room under 3ft of water, and the station under 4ft. Services were stretched to the limit, and support was drawn in from across Sussex.

Lifeboats and coastguard resources came in from the coast, Brighton, Eastbourne, even one boat from as far as Poole in Dorset.

The railway station looked more like a canalside as the water filled the tracks to platform level. Major and minor roads around were blocked by floodwater and abandoned cars. The official advice was simply "don't travel", and a spokesman for the fire brigade, which was trying to deal with rescues from property, rescues from cars, and road accidents, said: "It's chaos."

Lifeboats and coastguards came in from the coast – Eastbourne, Brighton and even one boat from as far as Poole in Dorset. Some residents escaped with only the clothes they stood up in

Water baby Harry Noah who would not wait

Further upstream more drama unfolded. At Hamsey farmer John Harmer, his wife Susan, and their two dogs, were airlifted to safety by a Solent coastguard helicopter, after being cut off by floodwater in a field with their herd of cows.

Expectant mum Julia Black from Barcombe almost had a rather different water birth for her baby than planned. Her contractions began at the height of the floods, and she and boyfriend Neil Griffin had to start their 12-mile journey to Crowborough birthing centre across two flooded fields, on a farm tractor-trailer and then lifeboat.

All the time her contractions were increasing and Neil had visions of having to deliver the baby in the boat.

They were met by ambulance to finish a two-hour journey which would normally take 30 minutes. Julia was able to have the water birth she wanted and baby Harry Noah weighed in at 8lb 3oz, oblivious to the problems he'd caused.

Historic brewery under water for 36 hours

Picture: Nigel Bowles, John Connor Press Associates

Lewes' landmark 200-year-old independent brewery Harvey and Son was awash with 6ft of water for about 36 hours. A group of 19 staff were stuck in the building on an upper level, rescued with the help of a fireman's ladder and lifeboat, threading its way through floating barrel obstacles.

As the water drained out, the weekend began a solid nine days of cleaning up.

"It was like walking back into a bomb site," said head brewer and joint director Miles Jenner. "It was quite a sight to see where stuff ended up. There was a tremendous amount of muck and filth with sewage and diesel."

Other brewers like Shepherd Neame in Faversham helped with operations such as cask-washing and transport until Harveys recovered. With a package boiler brought in and water and yeast supplies declared safe, brewing began again on the following Sunday.

"On that day we had a lovely letter pushed through the door, saying the smell had lifted the town's spirits," said Mr Jenner. Normality had begun to return.

An aerial photo of Brooks Road industrial estate in Lewes, taken 24 hours after the River Ouse burst its banks.

The speed of the flood water in Spences Lane, Lewes, was overwhelming. It was already 5ft deep at this point on the afternoon of Thursday October 12. The owners of these houses, built high on banked gardens, hoped they would escape but the water continued to rise, seeping under the front doors and soaking carpets.

The view on October 13 from Coombe Road, Lewes, looking across a new lake at the back gardens of numbers 1 and 2 Cranmer Close. Home owners were unable to reach their properties, except by boat, until the following day. Dennis Saines and his family were evacuated by lifeboat as the waters rose. He returned the following morning to retrieve food and clothing for his two-month-old daughter Ruby.

Malling estate, Lewes, was completely cut off from the rest of the town with both access roads, and the only pedestrian route, under water. Properties in Malling Street were some of the most severely damaged, with diesel from the flooded Esso service station contaminating the water. Even rescue vehicles became stranded in floods which reached five or six feet deep in places. Round the corner the Tesco petrol station was also flooded. The Esso garage was shut for 5½ weeks.

A van became stranded in the rising waters in Spences Lane, Lewes. Although areas of Lewes, like Uckfield, suffer flooding each year, Spences Lane has only flooded once before in living memory. There were no houses on the land then, only farmland with drainage ditches as it is on the edge of floodplains. Many houses and commercial properties have since been built in the area including the Royal Mail sorting office which was under 10ft of water. Thousands of letters and parcels had to be destroyed because of bacterial contamination.

Hearts were broken, along with furniture and treasured possessions like these belonging to the Rousell family in Cranmer Close, Lewes, which had to be thrown out into gardens to await disposal at the tip. Many families were unable to salvage anything because the risk of contamination was too great. The Rousells and many other families could not move back for six months until their homes had been dried out and re-fitted. It was a scene repeated in Malling Street, Cliffe High Street, Morris Road and other areas of the Malling and Landport estates.

Maidstone watched and waited as river rose

Kent's county town of Maidstone watched and waited as the river Medway rose steadily at its centre, swollen with floodwater which began gathering miles upstream on the borders with Surrey and Sussex.

The mid-October deluge created the highest river level, as the water just about squeezed under the bridges.

Police headquarters at Maidstone was the base for gold control co-ordination of all the agencies involved in the emergency.

In a crisis meeting with the Environment Agency on October 12 it was decided to open the flood barrier at Leigh to let through some of the backed-up water before defences burst above Tonbridge.

The Medway was flowing 140 times greater than normal at 150 cubic metres per second.

This meant evacuation plans for villages lower down, including Yalding and Benover.

Buses and ambulances moved about 200 people into emergency accommodation in Cornwallis School in Maidstone, but many residents refused to leave their homes, setting up camp in upstairs rooms until the water subsided.

Soldiers from nearby barracks, including Royal Engineers, Gurkhas and Paratroopers, helped emergency services with the process.

In Maidstone the Lock Meadow area flooded, including the Crown Court car park, the market site which meant weekly trading was cancelled, and around the leisure complex, but as the buildings are on stilts there they escaped.

The Social Services car park in Bishops Terrace became under water rather than under ground and the Drakes pub was one of the worst affected buildings in the town.

During Friday 13th there were fears that the river boat Kentish Lady II would break free of her moorings and block the river bridge, upsetting the delicate balance of floodwater flow with possibly disastrous results. But this was averted when emergency services brought in a specialist by helicopter to secure the moorings.

Through Friday night and Saturday morning the Tovil area was on standby for evacuation, but the danger passed, and although the later two major storms around Hallowe'en and Bonfire Night brought new peaks to the Medway, Maidstone was not affected as much again.

Fears that the Kentish Lady II would break her moorings and block the flow of water under the bridge, causing more flooding in Kent's county town, led to the arrival of a specialist by helicopter in Maidstone to check the moorings.
Picture by Lewis Durham (Kent News and Pictures)

The Medway was flowing 140 times greater than normal – buses and ambulances moved about 200 people into emergency accommodation at Cornwallis School

Maidstone: Medway Subway lives up to its name as the river fills the underpass. Picture by Lewis Durham (Kent News and Pictures)

Splashing along: A couple of horse-riders make their way through the centre of Yalding.

River Eden rose to the brink three times

Residents in Edenbridge watched carefully as the water rose following a night of heavy storms.

Collectively Edenbridge crossed its fingers three times during the four weeks, and with sandbags at the ready three times got away with it as the River Eden rose to the brink but left the town barely touched.

The arch of the Great Stone Bridge virtually disappeared from view in the torrent, and to the east and west two big lakes formed as the water swamped the flood plain up to the defence embankments built after the 1968 floods, protecting the Tannery and Co-op area.

Water levels rose faster second time around, and the river lapped the walls of the Baptist Church buildings, sneaking into the lower end of the High Street through a courtyard behind the church on the east side of the road - stretching up to Honours Mill and flooding half a dozen low-lying shops.

On the other higher side of the road premises remained dry, but water leaked through the river wall and flooded behind Bradford's electrical shop.

Residents of Marlpit Hill and Crockham Hill were

The river lapped the walls of the Baptist Church buildings, sneaking into the lower end of the High Street through a courtyard

left without electricity in the October 29 storm, but run-off and drain failure caused more problems than the river, especially around the Pound Green junction of Lingfield Road and Crouch House Road where a temporary large pond developed.

On the Spitals Cross estate its community room was flooded and garages were cut off by waist-deep water.

Head waters of the Upper Medway were gathering force upstream of Ashurst on the Kent-Sussex border, as roads and fields were awash. The power of the water was clear as it boiled through the A264 road bridge. In the village homes closest to the railway bridge were worst hit as the river burst its banks, and the sports field vanished under a sheet of water.

Penshurst at the confluence of rivers Eden and Upper Medway saw the causeway road to Bidborough disappear under water just below the entrance to Penshurst Place, cutting another bus route into Tunbridge Wells.

Betty Velvick (left) and her sister Jo Trepte.

The village of Groombridge was cut in two and the village school had to close

Further east at Groombridge the River Grom cut the village in two as it overflowed across the road, with knee-deep water outside the entrance to Groombridge Place.

The visitor attraction was closed, its grounds waterlogged, and St Thomas School was shut as pupils were unable to cross the flood.

Pensioner Jo Trepte and sister Betty Velvick were rescued by firemen with a ladder from Birchden Forge in Forge Road as water reached 4ft indoors, and 2ft higher outside on October 12.

Heavy furniture and treasured belongings were overturned and books were left in four inches of mud in the sitting room when the water receded (pictured right).

The fridge freezer and contents floated down the garden and some doves in the single storey barn were drowned.

Downstream the valley below Fordcombe demonstrated the function of flood plains, and minor roads became impassable cutting bus routes to Tunbridge Wells on October 12.

Children who travelled in to several schools from Edenbridge and villages further east, were "rescued" by the buses taking the long route home, via the A21, then the A25 through Westerham to reach Edenbridge from the north.

Receptionist Bernadette D'Souza had a lucky escape on Walters Green Road in Fordcombe the day after the late October storm. She drove into a "large puddle" where her car died and started to drift with water up to the windows.

She dialled 999 on her mobile phone and was advised to climb on to the car roof, from which she was rescued soaked and cold by PCs Rory Niblock and Lee Oakley in a Land Rover, which also risked floating away like Bernadette's car.

The road between Penshurst and Fordcombe which was closed after the river burst its banks.

Control centre set up in Tunbridge Wells

A stock of 4,500 sandbags stored in a metal container had been available for immediate use in the Tunbridge Wells borough for the past six years, and the council contracted Roland Duke's company in Horsmonden to supply 3,000 sandbags to stem the floods across the rural areas. Six men filled 400 bags every two hours, using up four tons of sand in the process.

More than 700 calls in the first two days were received at the control centre set up by Tunbridge Wells Borough Council to help emergency services give advice to residents and supply sandbags.

Two weeks later the crisis centre was re-opened during the Hallowe'en storm and more than 650 residents called a hotline to report at least 70 trees down from 8pm on the Sunday onwards.

Chainsaw gangs worked through the next day to clear roads and pavements, while homes across the borough were among 60,000 Seeboard customers left without electricity - said to be the worst damage to the network since the 1987 hurricane.

Manning the phones at Tunbridge Wells Borough Council's flood emergency control centre - Denise Shortall, Michelle Coutts, Katie Williams, Louise Cogman and Richard Highgate.

Tonbridge: a town on the brink of disaster

The dam which saved Tonbridge can be seen clearly in this aerial photograph taken by Clive Warrender. Six million metres of murky water were held back by the Leigh flood barrier. Downstream are the homes and offices of Tonbridge which were spared major devastation by this remarkable feat of engineering.

Floodwater spread into The Botany, off Tonbridge High Street, and crept up to the On the Map sculpture by Paddock Wood artist Ev Meynell - ironically the steel and perspex work represents the River Medway.

People marvelled at the lakes which appeared overnight in Somerfield and Sainsbury's car parks and by the Angel Centre.

Schools around the area closed and youngsters, like the group below in the Angel Centre car park, took advantage of the unexpected holiday to have fun in the floods on Friday October 13.

For adults coping with the watery invasion there was not much fun.

At the Angel Centre Indoor Bowls centre there was more paddling and bailing than bowling, as about 14 volunteers battled to slosh out the flood from the nearby stream - only to suffer again at the end of the month.

Courier reporters Emily Pennink and Jennifer Pickering took up an invitation from boatyard owner Phil Hibbs to experience a trip over the lake occupying Tonbridge sports ground. It was a tranquil scene in the sunshine away from the angry torrent passing under the High Street, as football and rugby goalposts were marooned on what is normally a wide island of land between two water courses.

Tonbridge Swimming Pool had more water than it wanted as the river invaded, causing extensive damage, and a likely six-figure cost to return to normal.

Fish and debris were left in the outdoor pool and interconnected indoor baths, the underground passages and plant room were covered in sludge, and the kitchens had more than two feet of water – only the raised spa escaped.

Recovery was set back by the second swamping in a fortnight.

Lifeguards Laura McTurk and Michaela Allen, with duty manager Keith Rogers, were among staff who helped in the clean-up as there were no swimmers to watch and little prospect of the pool re-opening before Christmas.

Five Oak Green: third flooding in one year

No school for these youngsters, Lydia Sheard and Amber, Nils and Jasmin O'Hara, as the village of Five Oak Green became a focus for about 40 firefighters and eight emergency vehicles. Kent Fire Brigade reported more than 400 calls for help across the flood-hit areas of the county in the 30 hours up to 1pm on Friday October 13. Three weeks and two major storms later its recording system was struggling to keep up with the rate of incidents being handled by emergency personnel.

Residents of Five Oak Green took their third dose of flooding in the year as the October weather took its toll, facing more ruined carpets, furniture, insurance claims and redecoration, and there were renewed grumbles about the failure of drainage. Worst hit were Five Oak Green Road, The Forge and Willow Crescent. Village Stores and Post Office owners Patrick and Paulette Sheard moved their stock to safety at 4am as the waters rose, determined not to lose thousands of pounds again. From Hobbs and Harrison hairdressers Emma Harrison said the shop had only just finished redecorating from previous flooding.

East Peckham: Army helped with evacuation

Milkman Bryan Oakley embodied village determination to carry on normal life as far as possible as he waded through Snoll Hatch Road in East Peckham. People barricaded their homes against water and used sandbags issued by army officers who were checking up on residents.

Waterlogged: Mattress barricade against the water in Snoll Hatch Road, East Peckham.

Roads were passable with care, but inflatable boats were used elsewhere in East Peckham. Units on Bainbridge's industrial estate looked like islands in the water. Old Road was badly affected, including the Rose and Crown pub, but undeterred locals donned wellies and waterproofs to wade to the Man of Kent pub.

The army turned up with inflatable boats to help out at East Peckham.

From the air the floodwaters could be clearly seen threatening the site of the Hop Farm Country Park at Beltring beside the A228.

Parts of nearby Paddock Wood did not escape, with some unlucky residents having to mop up, like George Cowderoy (right) perched on sandbags at his front doorstep in Maidstone Road, where nearby fields were under water.

Paddock Wood farmer Neil Wilson had a close shave when he went to check on his flock of sheep at Robertsbridge.

Rescue services were called out when he became marooned in a field with 78 of his animals.

He managed to wade out to higher ground through chest-deep fast-flowing water.

Two inflatable rescue boats were on hand but it was decided there were too many sheep to transfer in such a small craft and they were left stranded.

Farmer's mercy mission for sick child

Trainee teacher Kim Lowden and family from Collier Street were trapped in their home by 4ft of water on Hallowe'en morning, with one of the three boys ill with flu symptoms and a temperature of 102F.

Kim dialled 999 and then turned to neighbouring sheep farmer Andy Sanders and his tin boat for help. Andy had ferried two of the children over waist-deep water to dry land by the time Marden and Larkfield firemen arrived to complete the rescue, while neighbour Dorothy Highwood captured the scene on camera.

Changing landscapes: a field on Maidstone Road, Paddock Wood, is virtually under water.

Hop gardens near Goudhurst were under water as villages across the Weald of Kent were hit, keeping fire crews busy with calls after the October storms. These included helping motorists stuck in cars, and farmers seeking livestock stranded around Staplehurst and Marden, caught out by the speed of rising water. At Slaney Farm on the road to Headcorn farm worker John Lewis with a group of volunteers, waded waist-deep to move sheep to one of the few unflooded fields. Staff of several firms based in redundant farm buildings worked late to rescue office equipment. Further along cars were submerged in the road, made impassable even for four-wheel drive vehicles and lorries as the river Teise burst its banks.

A Range Rover successfully makes its way through the water on the Headcorn Road.

Cottage suffers both fire and floods

The fire damage to Forstal Farm in Newhouse Lane, Headcorn, where floods made access difficult for fire crews.

Firefighters were called to flooded cottages in Ulcombe Road, Headcorn, when the River Beult burst its banks after the mid-October deluge.

Then, a fortnight later, in the early hours of Hallowe'en morning they had to battle through four feet of water to reach a centuries-old farmhouse in New House Lane.

The home of widow Jane Bracher, flooded for the second time in two weeks, suffered a blaze in the roof at the rear which was dealt with by 30 firemen in six fire appliances.

Officers had to be ferried to the scene by fire engine because the water was too deep for their cars.

The Bonfire Night storm was another busy time. Cranbrook, Tenterden and Hawkhurst fire crews were called to pump out properties in Lamberhurst, then the Old Cloth Hall cellars flooded in Biddenden and a house in Benenden had three feet of water in its basement.

Hawkhurst crew worked with Seeboard to make safe electricity cables arcing at a row of cottages in Sandhurst Cross the previous evening.

Kent Air Ambulance helped Headcorn firefighters find an elderly woman sitting waist-deep in water trapped in her car by the River Beult in Water Lane.

The helicopter spotted her and circled overhead while the firemen reached the rescue scene.

Fire officers had to be ferried to the scene by fire engine because the water was too deep for their cars

Torrents of water flooded gardens on a Sissinghurst housing estate, bringing complaints from the Skinners Gardens residents about raw sewage as the water ran off higher ground behind the houses.

Flower beds and shed floors were awash and the level came within a whisker of breaching front doorsteps.

Staff at the National Farmers Union offices at Marden handled a steady stream of claims, many under household policies and from car drivers who had made the mistake of trying to make it through the floods.

Lamberhurst: village street became a river

The Chequers in Lamberhurst, (right) and landlady Claire de Garston (above).

Lamberhurst High Street became an extension of the River Teise on October 12, closing the busy A21 to traffic, and bringing TV crews to capture pictures which joined those of Uckfield to be shown live on news bulletins.

Some residents were stuck upstairs and others came to stand at the water's edge and stare in disbelief.

The village school was closed as white water rapids surged down the main street and one firefighter described their task as "like bailing out the Titanic with a teacup".

The force of the water shifted bottle banks and recycling containers and ripped up the surface in the Chequers Inn car park, tearing away half-barrel planters and window boxes as well.

Shops affected included Coggers greengrocers, Jill Hall's hairdressers where the floor was left covered in silt, and the Lexus car dealership showroom under feet of water. Some cars were water-damaged, but staff "risked life and limb" to move vehicles worth thousands of pounds out to higher ground.

Inspecting the damage at the Chequers car park barman Michael Osborne checked the drains. Inside the building the water had reached halfway up the bar and filled the cellar, wrecking pumping and cooling equipment.

For landlady Claire de Garston it was the fourth flood she had experienced in 18 months at the pub and she had not long finished redecorating after the previous two (in May and at Christmas). The latest damage was estimated at £40,000.

The Chequers was open for business in two weeks, only to be submerged again two days later after the Hallowe'en storm.

Claire stayed closed on the Monday, unable to face customers, and at the end of the week left for a holiday in Australia with her daughter, as far from the floods as possible.

She admitted she would love to leave the pub, but has invested too much money in it to walk away.

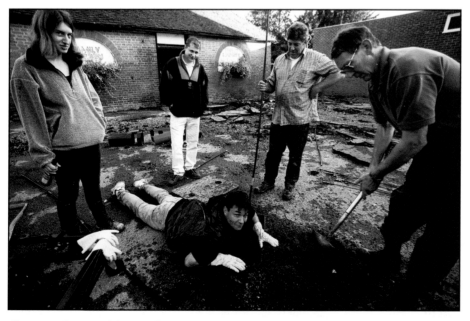

Chequers barman Michael Osborne checks a drain as part of the clean-up operation following the floods.

The river at Lamberhurst is close to bursting its banks again on October 30.

Here we go again! The River Teise rose rapdily at the end of October, but did not quite equal its previous performance. It drowned the garden at the George and Dragon Inn on the Broadway, which had escaped the worst a fortnight earlier with only the cellar flooded, thanks to the efforts of firefighters.

The Teise was angry and swollen with storm debris. The mid-October storm swamped the playing fields in Lamberhurst and left the car park under four feet of water.

An Alsatian dog tries to decide whether to brave the depths of the water which was flowing through Yalding.

Yalding: the centre of media attention

Rescuers getting ready to launch their boat to help residents of Yalding.

Yalding became the centre of media attention as it vanished beneath the waters of the Medway, Teise and Beult.

While other towns and villages across Kent and Sussex saw the floods recede, poor Yalding seemed to be submerged for most of the month. Each time the residents saw the water levels drop more rain raised them again.

Newspaper and TV journalists threatened to outnumber residents and the village was dubbed the unluckiest in England.

Emergency services and the army were called in to help and most routes into the village were blocked.

Some people waded through the flood with belongings in binliners. Boats were of most use in many places to evacuate those residents who did not stay put upstairs in their homes. Kent Fire Brigade had two boats of its own and others were called in from elsewhere.

Staff from Zeneca Agrochemicals organised a dinghy rescue service on October 13 with the owner of Hampstead Leisure and Marine Park to rescue people and pets from mobile homes.

Widower Fred Grainger had only 10 minutes to gather treasured possessions in three carrier bags. The Hampstead Park residents vowed they would stay together as a community, even if they could not return to the site.

Pensioner Roger Dugdale, his wife Phyllis and spaniel Daniel, were among evacuees, threatened with flooding for the first time in 22 years, while Mark

Newspaper and television journalists almost outnumbered the residents

It was an uphill struggle for this truck near Yalding Station but it did get through.

Hoare and partner Julie Watts spent two days stranded upstairs with their children, without heat and living on crisps and by candlelight. They watched logs, even a bench and table float past in the strong currents.

Caught on camera: Lyngs Close, Yalding, resident Joe Fenwick was filmed making his way home from the shops during the second phase of flooding, having been evacuated after the initial deluge. In the centre of the village at Bridge Cottage, near the 15th century ragstone bridge, David Boud and wife Margaretta had their home repeatedly swamped under several feet of water. The Edwards family, living by Yalding Bridge, were evacuated for four days when their 18th century Grade II-listed house was six feet deep in water, were clear for a week and then suffered another four-foot deep flood.

Another Lyngs Close resident, Richard Williams, takes a look at the wellie-height water near the George in Yalding after the Hallowe'en storm. By this stage some of the community were beginning to worry about insurance payouts arriving in time to refurbish for Christmas. Opposite the Orchard Stores Barry and Christine Reynolds said the sewage-contaminated water had wrecked their home to the tune of £15,000.

These French windows in Yalding beside the old packhorse bridge became a familiar sight on television news and came to symbolise the plight of the village. The dark line on the brickwork shows the high water mark of previous flood water.

This house is sitting in about three feet of water as the river submerges the centre of Yalding village.

One man and his boat. Edward Raikes heads home from the shops near the George, past houses sandbagged above their doorsteps against the invasion of nature. Doctors from the Bower Mount Surgery in Yalding ran their practice from a house in the village after the first flood, moving equipment and patient records upstairs for safety. Health minister John Hutton visited in November to congratulate them on their resourcefulness.

Sandbags are piled high against the front doors of Kingsland Cottages to try to provide some protection against the flood water which swept through Yalding over a period of several weeks.

Wateringbury: severe weather stops picnics

Fields near Wateringbury were awash with Medway water.

This picnic site near Wateringbury provided the understatement of the year with its sign saying: "Site closed due to severe weather conditions".

Lewes from the air with the swollen Ouse flowing into the town on the morning of Friday, October 13.

Sainsbury's and the Angel Centre car parks under water on Friday October 13 in Tonbridge.

More flood news inside: See pages 2, 4, 5, 6, 8 and 35

Uckfield edition

Flood warnings on the web

■ Latest road and rail news
■ Local school and other public services affected
■ Latest flood news and weather reports

Keep in touch
www.thisiskentandeas sussex.co.uk

The Courier

Established in 1872   Friday, October 13, 2000   45p

Reporting life in Blackboys, Framfield, Maresfield, Nutley, Ridgewood and local villages

McFLOOD: A view of McDonald's from Uckfield town centre at the height of the flooding yesterday   Photo: Courier reader Norman Rogers

Floods havoc

COASTGUARDS airlifted a man to safety after he was swept away as the worst floods in living memory hit Uckfield yesterday (Thursday) morning.

Dozens of shops were flooded and roads were impassable as the River Uck burst its banks for the second time this year.

By Faith Lee

In the town centre two men, Ian Shears, 25, and his friend, Bill Chapman, 23, plucked a woman to safety as she slipped while trying to walk to work through the floodwater at 6.15am.

Ian said: "We were trying to see if we could get through to get our lift to work.

"There was an elderly lady behind trying to get to work on the industrial estate.

"She put her foot down a drain where the cover had lifted and was submerged. I jumped and grabbed hold of her and we pulled her out."

They said the lady went home very shaken, but otherwise unhurt.

Firemen from Heathfield helped ambulancemen rescue an elderly lady from the second floor of Millington Court retirement home in Mill Lane.

They said the lady had been injured the following day, not connected with the floods, but needed to be taken to hospital.

The ground floor of Millington Court was partially under water with Mill Lane complete flooded.

Hundreds of people got an unexpected day off work and took the opportunity to go out and view the drama.

And for the second time this year Uckfield's flooded High Street featured on national television. Cars at Caffyns garage were under water and water had seeped into the main showroom among the new Rover 25 and 45 models on show.

One car's windscreen wipers had been set off by the floods and were working uselessly in the submerged car. Two cars were swept from Mill Lane into the High Street, almost completely submerged.

Mr Shears and Mr Chapman, tree surgeons for Brockwells Forestry which works for Seeboard, described seeing food, including fresh chickens floating out of Somerfield's store.

Windows smashed

Flood water smashed windows of Somerfield and washed hundreds of pounds worth of food out into the street where it was trapped against the railings.

The windows of Blockbusters video shop were smashed by the force of the water.

Residents of Keld Avenue woke up to find their cars under water with car alarms going off.

Police said they had no reports of injuries but roads were closed including the Uckfield bypass, Uckfield High Street and Framfield Road near the hospital.

RNLI from Eastbourne helped evacuate shops and industrial premises.

Mark Robinson of Eastbourne lifeboats said at lunchtime they were checking to make sure no-one was still trapped.

Man airlifted to safety after being swept away

A MAN nearly drowned after being swept away in the worst flooding to hit Uckfield in 50 years yesterday (Thursday).

Police said the man was seen to be carried away after clinging to a door of a shop at about 7.20am.

Twenty minutes later he was spotted conscious and shivering several hundred yards downstream by police and airlifted to the Princess Royal Hospital, Haywards Heath, by coastguards.

Chris Davies, of Anvil Close alerted emergency services when he heard the man calling for help.

He said: "I was walking back from MPE Electronics where I work, because it was shut, along a back road.

"I could hear someone very distressed calling help me, help me. I found him almost outside my back door. Behind my house there is a railway ravine and he was stuck on a island in the middle. He was wet and shaking. I tried talking to him but he did not seem to be taking it in.

"My wife called the police. Two of my neighbours came out. Then the helicopters arrived."

The man is said to be in a stable condition.

Police advised people to stay in their homes as the heavy rain made almost every road in the county impassable.

Almost all schools in Crowborough and Uckfield were closed. Clarissa Featherbee, teacher at Uckfield Community College said: "There are teachers in wellies trying to get water out of the building. We are going to be shut for the rest of the day and probably for a few days after that."

Eastbourne and Brighton coastguards sent inflatable craft to Uckfield after a request from the town's firecrew.

Residents, evacuated from their homes, were taken to Utopia Leisure Centre, as the hospital was unreachable and flooded.

Areas in the Rother Valley were also flooded including Station Road in Robertsbridge, as well as fields in Stonegate near the Cuckmere River.

THE COURIER'S AUTUMN BRIDES 2000 TAKES PLACE ON SUNDAY. FULL DETAILS ON PAGE 32

Courier staff produced a special flood edition less than 24 hours after the first disaster occurred at Uckfield. The following week the paper produced a 16-page flood supplement on the devastation throughout West Kent and East Sussex as the rain continued to fall.

Flooding in the Medway Valley

1880 - Watchers outside the Angel Hotel see Tonbridge High Street turned into a river

The Medway Valley, glorious in spring, serene and lovely in summer, so often turns on her admirers in the autumn and winter, pouring flood water into town and village, challenging man's puny attempts to push the river's flow along a defined course.

Tonbridge, the only large town in the upper Medway, has suffered for centuries and holds the key to what happens further downstream. There must be some sympathy with this year's claim that protecting Tonbridge and its flood-prone industries condemned Yalding, precariously situated at the confluence of three rivers, to be "the drain hole of Kent". Keep Tonbridge dry, say the critics, and villages downstream are bound to be inundated, as they have been this year.

Writers in the past said that Tonbridge "has had flooding since 1740". The date may be significant as the year the Medway was made navigable down to Maidstone, requiring a series of locks to ease the passage of barges. There was joy when the first cargo was unloaded at the Great Bridge, and soon barges were plying to and fro, sending down loads of Kent oak and produce from the Garden of England and returning with lime and stone to modernise a mainly wooden town. So the river "awoke to life" in the 18th century and Tonbridge grew and prospered. As the old town centred on church and castle expanded, caution

After suffering centuries of flooding, Tonbridge now gets the blame for being protected while the villages downstream are inundated

decreed that the first new houses should be located as far as possible from the river, as in Meadow Lawn, formerly called the Blue Barn Lands.

The High Street and the little roads adjoining it flooded almost every winter, often disastrously, when the hand-operated sluices in the old Hayesden Weir had to be drawn to let its penned-up water go.

The barge-owning Medway Company, excused from rates and taxes by Act of Parliament and ruling the river from Tonbridge downstream, was little help, being generally condemned as capricious, autocratic and oppressive. Selfish was the term most people used for directors said to be "coming very near to sainthood" in the early nineteenth century.

They were riding for a fall after the railway came to

1900 - A member of the Norton family of boatbuilders paddles to the rescue along Barden Road.

1891 - Through the flood by horse and cart.

1968 -The only fun in Barden Road, Tonbridge, was for boys in their boats.

Tonbridge in 1842 and took most of their trade. They cared nothing for the locks and bridges they controlled below the town, and in summer regularly penned sewage-laden water in Tonbridge's four tributary streams to keep their barges afloat. Autumn storms regularly poured water into the narrow ill-paved Tonbridge High Street, bringing misery to cottagers in and around Lamberts Yard and to shops built below road level.

Shopkeepers in the lower High Street kept "flood boards" ready to seal their doorways when water crept up from the town's natural flood plain embraced by two arms of the Medway. This was the Racecourse, renamed the Sports Ground when the council bought it in 1923. It is still Tonbridge's front line protection when, as local people say, "the floods are up".

Over the years the floods claimed several lives. None shocked the town more than the drowning of Joseph Featherstone, a master baker, swept away in the swollen river while taking his horse for a drink in the "Wash" beside the Great Bridge. Many people saw it

happen but were unable to help. On the recommendation of a coroner's jury, posts and chains were erected to separate the so-called Horsewash from the main stream. Eventually the shallow part was filled in and incorporated into the Lower Castle Walk.

Instead of alleviating flooding by managing its locks in the public interest the Medway Company stood aloof while pursuing endless litigation in defence of what it saw as its rights. In 1910 a receiver was appointed and a new company attempted to restore the Medway traffic. But it was too late and when the East Farleigh lock collapsed due to years of neglect the river had to be closed to traffic.

Alarm spread along the whole Medway Valley and after a series of public meetings and many bitter recriminations Kent County Council stepped in and appointed Medway Conservators to buy out the old shareholders and reconstruct the river, a task that took five years and cost three times the £30,000 estimate.

Tonbridge secured some relief when as part of this

1911 - Crowds gather to watch the rising water in Tonbridge on November 19.

1911 - Also taken on November 19, this picture shows the High Street looking north.

work the Town Lock was rebuilt with the addition of broad by-pass channel. But even this obvious alleviation was not easily achieved, requiring the rejection of at least six schemes before one was agreed.

Arthur Neve in his book The Tonbridge of Yesterday published in 1933 wrote: "It is perhaps too much to say there will be no more floods in the town, but it may be safely asserted that as a result of the improvements carried out under the Medway Conservancy Act of 1911 the risk has been reduced to a minimum." How wrong he was.

Hayesden Weir, highly regarded in summer as a place for swimming and camping, offered no real protection against winter storms. Water got into the High Street whenever the river overflowed. One of the most miserable floods occurred in the spring of 1947 when the country, exhausted after six years of war, was just emerging from weeks of ice and snow. Heavy rain following a sudden thaw poured off the deeply frozen ground and into homes and businesses. A glorious summer followed.

Walls built along the River Walk in 1958 were more or less successful in keeping the Medway in its course until October 1968, when heavy and persistent rain draining into an already swollen river sent a torrent into the High Street. Upstream Edenbridge also suffered badly and villages downstream were overwhelmed.

Tonbridge has been protected since 1981 by the Leigh flood barrier which holds millions of gallons of flood water behind a high earth dam until it is safe to let it go in a controlled flow. Lucky for Tonbridge, but sad for Yalding, Laddingford and East Peckham when the tidal Medway backs up below Maidstone and merges with the Teise and Beult.

1968 - A double decker bus on its way to Uckfield ploughs its way through the choppy waters in Tonbridge.

1968 - An alarming moment in Tonbridge as the river bursts its banks.

The high flood at Penshurst on February 16, 1900, as water rushes across the causeway. See page 40 for the 2000 version.

These floods caused problems in Edenbridge in 1958 but were only a warning of worse to come a decade later

Edenbridge has lived with the threat of flooding since the beginning of the 20th century

Residents of Edenbridge have lived with the threat of flooding since the beginning of the 20th century. The River Eden runs through the low lying town centre and has burst its banks on a number of occasions.

The floods of 1958 caused problems in the town but were only a warning of what would happen 10 years later.

In October 1968 the Eden burst its banks in what was to be the town's worst flood disaster of the century. The water covered a large area of the town close to the bridge forcing many businesses to close and residents to be evacuated.

Hever Castle was under more than 4ft of water, tractors were used to rescue people and emergency supplies were flown in by an army helicopter.

In this instance the town suffered more than Tonbridge and when the flood barrier was built at Leigh, residents feared that Edenbridge would be put at greater risk.

So far, however, these fears seem to be unfounded with floods never reaching their 1968 high water mark and only seriously affecting properties close to the bridge on the High Street.

How Sussex has coped in the past

The Keymarket store in Uckfield was flooded again – for the third time in two years – on the morning of November 22, 1974. About a third of the stock was ruined and shops in the area suffered damage running into thousands of pounds.

One High Street shop had to throw out about a ton of greengroceries. Water near the bus station was about two feet deep when the petrol tanker in the photograph ploughed its way through.

Robertsbridge experienced more flooding, but at Etchingham luck was with commuters who left their cars at the railway station. The water stopped a few feet short of the vehicles.

One Uckfield shop had to throw out about a ton of greengroceries when in November 1974 the river Uck burst its banks for the third time in two years

No fun at this fair…Damage expected to amount to more than £2,000 was caused when floods inundated a travelling fair at Bell Brook Meadow, Uckfield, on Saturday May 17, 1975. Valuable equipment was swamped in up to three feet of water when the River Uck burst its banks once again. Fairground workers toiled throughout the day, sometimes wading waist deep in water, to get their machinery out as the river threatened to rise again - but most of it was rendered useless. Smaller items were swept away, including the fair's stock of light bulbs.

Gale force winds coincided with the highest tides for many years on February 11, 1974, and the River Uck, a tributary of the tidal Ouse, rose to dangerous levels. At 4am police found that at Hempstead Mill, the lowest point along the river bank, the mill race was so full that water threatened to burst through the floor of the mill, a private residence. They helped the family to evacuate the ground floor and sandbagged the front door and the French windows.

Three hours later the river burst its banks behind the Keymarket store at the bottom of the High Street. Water flooded the car park, built up against the walls of the store, and began to seep under the doors. Police called out the manager and helped him to clear some of the lower display shelves as four inches of flood water swept through the store and out into the street. But Keymarket stayed open.

The other side of the picture – the November 1974 flood in Uckfield's lower High Street, looking towards the Bridge Hotel, now the Cock and Bull, and the original site of the railway station.

On the same day that housewives were paddling while they shopped at Uckfield's Keymarket store, police and farm workers rescued 160 in-lamb ewes at Little Buckham Farm, Isfield. The sheep had been driven into a valley by gales and then trapped when the River Ouse overflowed. The ewes were taken to safety in a boat borrowed from the police cadet section at Lewes.

One of the lanes between Burwash Common and Stonegate disappeared under water in May this year.

A Land Rover makes its way through the water near the level crossing in Etchingham in May this year.

The Sussex rivers are uneasy neighbours

The Sussex rivers Rother, Ouse, the Uck and the upper Medway have always been uneasy neighbours for those who live and work near their banks - and particularly the normally placid Uck, which has so often burst its banks and flooded the lower part of Uckfield High Street.

It is not a new problem for Uckfield. A map of 1784 shows that there were "clappers" - raised walkways for pedestrians - on the town side of the river bridge, one of the areas most vulnerable to flooding, and an adjacent meadow is shown as Clappers Mead.

At the end of the 18th century two men standing near the bridge were swept away by the torrent and drowned.

The Uck - a relatively recent name, for the river is shown on old maps as the Ouse, of which it is a tributary - flooded in January 1918, November 1929, January 1939, January 1943, November 1952, November 1960, February and November 1974, and December 1993.

The floods of 1960 were said to be the worst the town had experienced for more than 40 years.

The water rose so rapidly that people living or working in the area had little time in which to act. Shop owners saw their stock floating away down the street. Crates of beer were awash in the Bell Hotel's cellars, and trains stopped running between Uckfield

Flooding is not a new problem for Uckfield - a map of 1784 shows raised pedestrian walkways on the town side of the river bridge

and Lewes because the track was unsafe. There was 18 inches of water between the platforms at the railway station, and it took four men to close the level crossing gates against the surging water.

Fourteen years later the river rose again when gale force winds and heavy rain coincided with the highest tides for 300 years, flooding acres of farmland, several roads, and the Keymarket store in the High Street, the ground floor of Uckfield Mill, and Mill Lane itself.

The lower High Street from Bell Lane to a point near the level crossing was under two feet of water, and there was flooding at Coopers Green and on the road to Framfield, where planks were laid over a flooded playground to enable children to get to school.

Police used a 14-foot dinghy to rescue 160 sheep

Uckfield Mill surrounded by water in 1943, one of the major flooding incidents in Uckfield's history during the 20th century. In those days the mill was owned by E. Warburton and Sons and was a working corn and oat mill.

marooned at Little Buckhams Farm, Isfield.

In November of the same year the Keymarket store was flooded again, and about a third of the stock was ruined. Altogether, shops suffered damage running into thousands of pounds.

There was a lull for about 20 years - and then the floods returned, inundating the lower High Street and the Lo Cost supermarket in particular. While a few people were questioned by police investigating reports of looting, others, total strangers, waded into the flood to help shopkeepers rescue whatever could be saved. The Anchor Inn at Barcombe was cut off by the swollen River Ouse, but patrons, determined not to be beaten, arrived by boat.

The cellars of the White Hart at Buxted were flooded, and a house next door had three feet of water in the ground floor.

The 1947 floods which followed heavy snowfall seem to have had little impact on East Sussex, although in March the Kent & Sussex Courier published a photograph of a youth paddling his home-made canoe in a meadow near Stonegate station.

But in 1960 it was a different matter, and on November 3 the previous month's record rainfall wrought havoc. Parts of Lewes were flooded, elderly folk were marooned in cottages at Eridge, where the the cellars, dining room and kitchen of the Huntsman pub were three feet under water. At the nearby railway station water lapped within 18 inches of the platforms.

In 1974 the Rother went on the offensive. Low-lying fields in the Etchingham and Robertsbridge area were flooded to a depth of two feet. Houses in Robertsbridge High Street suffered, and the village recreation ground became a lake. At Etchingham the water stopped a few feet short of commuters' cars parked at the railway station.

The Rother burst its banks at Bodiam in the following year. Continuous heavy rain caused the closure of several roads in East Sussex and fields were flooded, but damage to property was only slight. Robertsbridge's recreation ground disappeared under water once more, but houses escaped.

It was a disastrous year for a travelling fair which visited Bellbrook Meadow at Uckfield. The river rose unexpectedly one night in May, and valuable equipment disappeared under three feet of water, causing damage of something like £2,000.

In 1990, following a mini-hurricane which left East Sussex County Council with a £1.3 million bill for repairing schools, other buildings and roads, the Uck repeated its by now familiar routine and burst its banks, this time flooding the road at the bottom of Buxted Hill.

The River Rother burst its banks in February 1974, flooding houses in Robertsbridge High Street, the village's recreation ground, and meadows in the area. Cars were submerged at Etchingham, but there was no loss - they were all wrecked vehicles and had already been taken off the road.

Floods spread across fields near Groombridge, close to the spot where, 40 years earlier, an elderly couple who were marooned in their car under a railway bridge had managed to attract the attention of the driver of an approaching train and had then been guided to safety and drier land up the railway embankment.

It's all happened before...

Flooded fields between Withyham and Groombridge in January 1990.

The upper Medway and its tributaries have often flooded meadows between Hartfield, Withyham and Groombridge, but 10 years ago the results were more spectacular than usual. A Courier photographer took this picture of flood waters swirling across submerged fields near Groombridge.

January 1975 and the River Rother bursts its banks again. This was the scene near the bridge at Bodiam.

capture the memory

Firemen provide supplies for Eridge families

Clothes props have many other uses - and this one came in handy for a Crowborough fireman to pass a shopping bag containing a flask of tea up to a resident of Mount View, Eridge, marooned upstairs by flood water in November 1960.

One couple declined to be rescued, preferring to stay where they were until their daughter arrived from London. The firemen also supplied other families with food and warm clothing.

At Groombridge a train crew rescued two people trapped in their car under a railway bridge. They managed to attract the driver's attention and were helped up the embankment to safety.

Elsewhere there was trouble on the line - a train was stopped not far from Rotherfield station when a bank, weakened by heavy rain, collapsed and earth slid across the track.

Flood water rose to within 18 inches of the platforms at Eridge station, but the steam-hauled trains kept running.

"Nice to see you…" A welcoming smile from one of the occupants of Mount View, Eridge, marooned by the November 1960 floods, as a Crowborough fireman climbs to check on their safety.

When residents in Mount View, Eridge, were marooned in 1960 a Crowborough fire crew came to the rescue – with tea and shopping

Contents

Acknowledgements	2
Introduction	3-5
Diagram of flooded areas	4
Weather	6-7

Uckfield
McDonald's	3
PC wades to work	5
Aerial picture	8
October 12 torrent	9
Vehicles submerged	10
Jeweller rescued	11
Prince Edward's visit	11
Emergency services	12
Cock and Bull pub	13
Somerfield food afloat	14
Signal box at sea	15
Peacocks clothes line	15
Wet floor humour	16
Mini survivor	16
Watching the water	17
Bell Walk damage	18
Coracle transport	19
Flood saviours	20
Bell Walk aftermath	21
Bridge Cottage	22
Uckfield Mill	23
Rescue on video	24
Cafe clean-up	24
Flooding history	71-78

Buxted and Framfield
Rural road collapse	25
New lake appears	25

Stonegate and Burwash
Road cut, farm flood	26

Etchingham
Station canal scene	26
Wet rail parking	27
Ancient church suffers	28

Robertsbridge
Rain stops play	29

Lewes
Rescuers at risk	30
Ouse swamps town	31
Water baby Harry Noah	32
Brewery rescue	33
Aerial view of Harvey's brewery	34
Spences Lane	34
Boating return home	35
Petrol station swamped	35
Malling estate roads	36
Aerial picture	**Inside back cover**

Maidstone
Kentish Lady II drama	37
Subway submerged	38

Edenbridge
Scene from Stone Bridge	39
Past floods	70

Ashurst
Upper Medway overflows	40

Penshurst
Joined rivers cut road	40

Groombridge
Village cut in two	41

Fordcombe
Escape from car roof	42

Tunbridge Wells
Borough control centre	43
Sandbag delivery	43

Leigh
Flood barrier aerial view	44

Tonbridge
Botany and Angel Walk	45
Sportsground boating lake	46
Swimming pool clean-up	46

Five Oak Green
Firefighters fight floods	47

East Peckham
Milkman delivers pinta	48
Doorstep barricades	48
Army rows in to help	49

Beltring
Hop Farm park	50

Paddock Wood
Farmer marooned	51
Maidstone Road	50-51

Collier Street
Mother and sons rescued	51

Goudhurst and Weald villages
Hop fields under water	52

Headcorn
Floods and fire rescues	53

Lamberhurst
A21 and Chequers flooded	54
Second time around	55
Soggy playing fields	56

Yalding
Riders splash out	38
Launch the lifeboats	57
Outside Orchard Stores	5 & 58
Famous French windows	59
Kingsland Cottages	60
Aerial picture	**Back cover**

Wateringbury
No picnics today	61

Aerial pictures
Tonbridge	**Inside front cover**
Uckfield	8
Harvey's Brewery	32
Leigh flood barrier	44
Lewes	62
Sainsbury's car park, Tonbridge	63
Lewes	**Inside back cover**
Yalding	**Back cover**

Courier headline news	64

Flooding history
Kent	65-70
Sussex	71-78

Photo order details	79